CW00421912

All Things Must Pass

A New Collection of

Contemporary Poems

by

Steve Langhorn

Introduction

In June 2020 I published my first book of poetry, Extraordinary Times, Extraordinary Rhymes. This was essentially a poetic narrative of living through the early stages of the Covid-19 pandemic written in the style of a diary, as events, thoughts and feelings unfolded day by day.

This follow-up continues in the same style, expressing my observation of not only the pandemic, but life in general. The title All Things Must Pass on the one hand is a message of hope that we will get through the current difficulties, but also the very nature of life as children grow and we all age.

I hope you enjoy reading the poems as much as I enjoyed writing them.

Acknowledgement to Matthew 24:6-8 in the Bible and George Harrison for the book title.

Thanks to Chris Stringer for designing the book cover.

Cover artwork courtesy of 'Yuri_Arcurs'

Copyright © 2020 Steve Langhorn

All rights reserved.

ISBN: 9798566455907

I would like to thank my family, not just for listening to, and positively commenting on my work, but also providing a great deal of the inspiration for the content.

A donation will be made to the Alzheimer's Society for every book sold:

Alzheimer's Society is the UK's leading dementia charity. We campaign for change, fund research to find a cure and support people living with dementia today. Dementia is the UK's biggest killer, and someone develops it every three minutes and there's currently no cure. Life with dementia is hard enough but 2020 has intensified the everyday challenges people living with dementia – and their carers - face. No-one could have anticipated the devastation that coronavirus would bring. In its wake, people affected by dementia have lost skills, confidence, and their connection to the world around them. Many feel a good life is no longer in their grasp. Alzheimer's Society's lifeline support services were the emergency service for people affected by dementia in the depths of the crisis – and they will be again during subsequent lockdowns. Dementia Advisers have supported grieving families, escalated safeguarding issues hidden behind closed doors and helped people to cope day by day

In aid of

1st June 2020

A rather light-hearted take on ageing.

1
When I'm 64

Get up now it's 8 o'clock
Stretch the body then take stock
Getting up too fast could cause concern
You might just take a dizzy turn

How many pees did I have last night
Too many times gives me a fright
Was that a muscle going in my back
Or am I just a hypochondriac

A sharp pain goes across my chest
Oh it's just a clothes peg stuck in my vest
I feel a pain in my left knee
It'll have to wait, I'm busting for a wee

That ache I get in my right shoulder
Is a sure sign I am getting older
No glasses on, my sight it fades
So I'm struggling to find my hearing aids

I work hard to avoid impending ills
By religiously taking my vitamin pills
Reducing the risk if there is any
But why do I take so bloody many

Now off to bed, we must behave
It's a good night's sleep I really crave
A nice hot cup of malted milk
And I drift off to sleep smooth as silk

3rd June 2020

My elder brother has lived in Australia since the 1970's. I wrote this poem in recognition of his 70th birthday

2
Seven Decades

Brought into the world in the dusk of war
The Langhorn family grows by one more
Not one to tolerate living in the limelight
Single-minded, always right

Lived the life his teenage kicks
Never turned his back on local conflicts
A temper that could quickly ignite
This boy always willing to stand and fight

A better life was there he reckoned
And a life down under always beckoned
For some years they had to wait
But eventually they got the leaving date

Along with their charming baby belle
Mum and Dad and little Michelle
A new life Australia quickly gave
Them their little paradise in Mulgrave

Along came Matt, and then they were four
A happy family could not ask for more
A daily challenge at the stove for Mummy
Trying to fill that growing boy's tummy

With city life they were done
Off to the coast in Mornington
A seaside town, a social hub
Lovely shops and of course the pub

New battles though soon came along
He had to be brave, he had to be strong
That spirit though will never fade
As he enters this new decade

20ᵗʰ June 2020

The news from America was regarding the death of
George Floyd was terrible but the reaction appeared
to me to be driving more division and dispel notions
of unity and equality.

3
All Lives Matter

A black man died in Minnesota
He did something he shouldn't oughta
People say he was drugged and high
But surely he didn't deserve to die

The footage flashed around the world
Accusations they were hurled
At the officers carrying out the arrest
The media storm they could not contest

No one should die like this, black or white
But a racist fire has been set alight
From history books to old statues
They're now all bad the crowds accuse

The marches they will surely end
When Twitter finds another trend
And what will all this hatred have achieved
Other than leaving all of us more aggrieved

A fairer society is a noble aim
Where opportunities are all the same
Surely we must address this social plight
But for everyone, not just black or white

6th July 2020

One morning whilst holidaying in Blakeney I took the dog for an early morning walk and was struck by what a beautiful location in was.

4
Postcard from Blakeney

Sunrise over the receding tide
A lovely place to rest and hide
From a constant barrage of gloomy news
As aggressive journalists express their views

A healthy breeze blows up narrow streets
Walking dogs and friendly greets
Pebbled houses with red rooftops
Local pubs and little shops

Spectacular views for all to see
The lapping waves of the Northern sea
The coastal car park starts to fill
The bacon butties keep out the chill

There is no place I'd rather be
Than in my place in my Blakeney
This joy from which we have been deprived
Now open the door, we have arrived!

16th July 2020

My brother, who is living with early onset Alzheimer's is undergoing a change in personality along with the obvious impact on his memory. I wrote this to remind myself what he used to be like.

5

The Quiet One

A gentle man with a friendly smile
Always willing to go the extra mile
To help his family gathered round
Without a fuss, hardly a sound

Gives himself to all the others
Wife and child, sister and brothers
All this done without a fuss
Seeks no thanks for helping us

He's not there you might assume
Often the quietest in the room
Never seeking a big audience
Steady of mood shows little variance

Inside there is still that man
Fighting that intruding bogeyman
Who twists his normal calm behaviour
The person we remember can be our saviour

Glimpses we still see of the gentle soul
Loved and cherished by us all
Enjoy that person whilst we can
And never forget he's still the quiet one

17th July 2020

One of my many musings about getting older.

6
Autumn Leaves

Life rattles on like a train
A brand-new spring comes round again
New experiences we behold
Never thinking we'll get old

Our parents passing is so sad
If they were old it's not too bad
As we're consoled with their good innings
And focus on kids and new beginnings

Our summers pass in a flash
As through our lives we hurry and dash
Every day so full and busy
Life in the fast lane makes us dizzy

But summers passed, it's getting cold
Friends and siblings start looking old
We're not immortal and one believes
Our time is short when Autumn leaves

17th July 2020

I used this to start a chapter in my autobiography,
particularly about the time I got a big promotion, with
all the trimmings!

7
Reach for The Sky

It happened so fast, took my breath away
You're now the boss with lots more pay
I thought I'd had a visit from Santa
Lots of cash and an Opel Manta

Embraced the role with relative ease
Thought I was the proverbial bees' knees
Working hard for what I earnt
Till the job just crashed and burnt

24th July 2020

I have been continuously amused, bemused and astonished at the position Donald Trump has assumed throughout the Covid-19 pandemic.

8

I Wanna Be Elected

(Title courtesy of Alice Cooper)

The American people are scared stiff
Whilst their President looks in the mirror and combs
his quiff
When it comes to balancing lives or earning dollars
It's all about jobs he constantly hollers

It's a problem with the numbers he attests
We are simply doing too many tests
With the lines on the graph going the wrong way
He's scared it's at the ballot box he will pay

It's as if he doesn't understand fully
That this is not a time he can bully
Living in constant denial
About the gravity of this trial

You might not like his arrogant persona
If you are living in Arizona
It's not so bad they are told
As cases increase daily six-fold

The truth you cannot sugar coat
He'll let people die to secure your vote
Another lockdown and all that pain
So he can make America 'grate' again

24th July 2020

My brother lives in Australia in the state of Victoria, which has been subject to very severe restrictions to control the outbreak of Covid-19 there. The State Premier did not make himself very popular in his handling of this situation, to say the least!

9
Victoria's Secret

We must put you in quarantine
I know you are not terribly keen
Fourteen days is all it lasts
Do not worry it will pass

We don't need police or army folk
The state Premier said in his talk
Despite the protests and the noise
He drafted in his bully boys

You can leave just don't be rash
You can do most things if you give me cash
There are other ways to win my favour
Especially if you are a little raver

Off they went free to shop
Coming and going, it was non-stop
Wandering round with consummate ease
To spread their worst with every sneeze

The consequences soon were pretty dire
Now Victoria, the Australian pariah
The virus rampant with increased infection
Hope this guy doesn't seek re-election

18th August 2020

I wrote this to celebrate the wedding of our good
friends' son, conducted under the Covid-19
conditions at that time.

10
Entente Cordiale

This is a day we could not miss
To be together in wedded bliss
A great big do was not allowed
The chosen few made up our crowd

A bijou gathering was prepared
The Doogan clan was undeterred
Surrounded by those who matter most
For our celebration and wedding toast

The bride stunning in her white dress
The groom looking his very best
Everybody behaved, no histrionics
Mum and Dad and even Onyx

Such warm emotions they arouse
As they exchange rings and wedding vows
So raise a glass and let's hail cheers
And wish them well for the coming years

18th August 2020

For those not familiar with Australia there is a well-known cheese brand called 'Coon' named after the man who launched it in 1935. The Company who owns the brand today are going to change the name because it has alleged racial implications.

11
Hard Cheese

It's gone too far there's no turning back
Next thing you know it will be Cilla Black
BLM now makes the rules
We just follow us silent fools

Speak carefully, don't say the word
You'll be arrested if you're heard
We now all playing the political game
Such that a dead man loses his name

Now when you shop it's not the same
Be careful when you choose a name
Don't dare buy that blackcurrant cake
The world's gone mad for goodness sake

Stock up now it's not too soon
To buy the cheese from William Coon
God help our future as we kowtow
Your every word is censored now

21ˢᵗ August 2020

I was reminiscing here on my times as an Area
Manager for an off-licence company in Central
Liverpool, interesting times.

12
Liverpool Lullaby

On street corners and down back alleys
That's were they lurk, the Liverpool Scallies
There not a pocket that isn't worth picking
No personal item that isn't worth nicking
All the tricks and bags of guile
They'll rob you blind with a smile
Rob your car, break in your house
Giving lip in distinctive scouse
Their bare face cheek is something to behold
But deep inside, they have a heart of gold

22nd August 2020

This was the opening verse for a chapter of my autobiography describing one of our many house moves.

13
Wherever I Lay My Hat

Leaving behind life by the sea
A way of life that wasn't to be
To familiar turf we must return
Going back home to good old Blackburn
Here is where the loneliness ends
Back amongst our family and friends

24th August 2020

Yet another form on lockdown, sadly this seems to be
the way things are going for the foreseeable future.

14
Déjà Flu

I woke this morning feeling deja vu
Another night another curfew
All that effort was just a waste
A normal life was just a fleeting taste

Those little things that we do cherish
Gone for now as people perish
Locked in here with just Sky news
Too much chatter and opposing views

We pass our time just counting the days
Till stupid people change their ways
Such precious time we wish away
With a cold beer or another cabernet

We will emerge from all this strife
To return to a kind of normal life
But for others there will be no such light
With life's struggles they must continue their fight

6ᵗʰ September 2020

Our good friends Andy and Gill had gone through a
very rough few months and decided to escape to
France for a few months to recuperate.

15
French Connection

The last few months have been pretty rough
And we decided we'd had enough
So without a fuss or song and dance
We packed the car and took off to France

Lots of stuff we had to sort
Even the dog needed a passport
A warning to you little French pooches
Our Amber doesn't do kisses and smooches

Our departure point still unknown
Is it Ashford or is it nearby Folkestone
But have no worries we caught the train
We'll soon be driving past the Seine

Sunny skies and lovely weather
But the main thing is we'll be together
Away from all the noise and chatter
Our time alone is what really matters

16th September 2020

A proud moment, my little grandson's first day at school.

16
First Day

I'm very excited I have to say
It's going to be a special day
This day will be without exception
As this big boy goes into reception

I love my teacher that's for sure
I know her name is Mrs Moore
All us kids are sure to behave
And as we leave we'll get a cheery wave

We must be good we are told
But remember I'm only four years old
But I am really not that small
I am actually forty six inches tall

Some might think I am daft
But I really do love doing my craft
Or if not I'll like to see
My favourite Number Blocks on TV

When I grow up I'd like to be
Something special, but let's just see
Maybe I could be a bread maker
Then I would 'Alfie Baker'

17th September 2020

When Covid regulations were eased in September it
was time to catch up with all those check-us that had
been cancelled in the previous months.

17
A Check-up from the Neck-up

We've been locked up for half a year
But now check-up time is coming near
With passing time a war I'm waging
To prevent my old body ageing

I'm rather worried by teeth are dirty
The dentist says he'll see me at two-thirty
He pokes and prods beneath my gums
And prizes out my breakfast crumbs

The optician can only see me at half past ten
I don't know what happens if you're not there then
After lots of tests and exploration
He says there's been no deterioration

The hearing test is a rather bigger task
I can't hear a word from behind that bloody mask
But she presses ahead rather half-cocked
And announces that my ears are blocked

Things had gone well, at least so far
Then I can't remember where I parked the car
Off with the mask, my hearing aid goes flying
Where the hell is it, I feel like crying

So, all in all I'm in reasonable fettle
I drive straight home and put on the kettle
The aging process held at bay
And fit to fight another day

17th September 2020

This was the day I was notified that my pension was going to be paid. I welcome the money but not the symbolism.

18
My Generation

A brown envelope popped through my door
Surely the taxman doesn't want any more
But of cash demands there was no mention
It was the Government offering me my pension
It's coming to me a year too late
But it's being old enough that I really hate
Each morning I look in the mirror and reflect
If there's signs of ageing I can detect
I check the certificate for year of birth
There could be an error for what it's worth
As the ink on there has begun to fade
There may be an error recording the decade
Old folks I know just moan and sigh
I just change my age and then just lie
Most days I feel like a twenty-year-old
My wife says I can look but cannot hold
That wasn't really what I meant
But I'm not the kind to cause an argument
As my hero Neil would always say
It's better to burn out than fade away

18th September 2020

Another of my rants at the media

19
Have I Got News for You?

Guaranteed to increase your stress
Watch TV, check your phone or read the press
They hype the story of the day
So for their news we continue to pay

As we increase Mr Murdoch's wealth
He in turn compromises our mental health
Where quality analysis is hijacked
Polished up and expressed as fact

The notion that they educate and inform
Has long since ceased to be the norm
We search for the truth to no avail
It's just a commodity up for sale

In this age of disinformation
They seek to create a bigger sensation
Balancing views is just not their way
Just a procession of moaners having their say

18th September 2020

This was a little ode dedicated to our old towing caravan that gave us so much pleasure when the kids were young.

20
Tow the Line

Our home in tow we hit the road
Around the UK, and even abroad
Whatever the weather, rain or shine
We were snug as a bug in our Fibreline
Although towing her weight was not too my liking
The grand old lady was our very own Viking

18th September 2020

I won't spoil the punchline in this verse

21
Washing Your Granny

The old lady is getting rather old
Groans a lot and hates the cold
Her paled colour looks rather worn
With passing years we watch and mourn
As she ambles down the road with great care
Venturing too far just isn't fair
She doesn't really wash, as such
So I don't really take her out that much
This situation I can't prolong
I know its harsh I know it's wrong
But things have really gone too far
It's time I purchased a new car

19th September 2020

We were so excited in our younger days to buy a brand-new house, it was the worst place we ever lived!

22
The House That Jack Built

For a while we thought we were dreaming
A brand-new house, all bright and gleaming
A lovely spot in a cul-de-sac
This was it, no turning back
All too soon we realized
The neighbours weren't that civilised
Donny and his foul-mouthed wife
Caused us pain, trouble and strife
A big mistake it was to prove
It was too much, we had to move

20th September 2020

My older brother who suffers from Alzheimer's with
its relentless and cruel impact has started to believe
his wife is holding him prisoner in the current
lockdown, I attempted here to imagine how he views
the situation.

23
Lockdown

I know you think it's all in my mind
The way that I am being confined
The windows closed the doors are barred
I can only wander in the yard

You subject me to interrogation
Just to increase my aggravation
What day is it, who's the prime minister
Your methods are increasingly sinister

I do not even know your name
Everyone out there just looks the same
Strangers pass before my eyes
I suspect they are more of your spies

Never knowing if it's night or day
If I get up in the dark there's hell to pay
I won't give up, I won't back down
I'm stronger than you, I won't breakdown

My friends in here will rescue me
And take me where I meant to be
I look in the mirror and I reflect
On an escape you will never even detect

My new disguise you think is weird
The unkempt look, the scruffy beard
I'm getting worse I think you fear
But it's just my plan to break out of here

You sit and think about the past
Our lives are now just a cruel contrast
Those memories you can disregard
I'm now just a prisoner and you're the guard

20th September 2020

Yet another set of rules to think about in tackling the
Covid-19 pandemic.

Warning: Contains Bad Language

24
'Deja Flu Two'

It's back again, it déjà vu
The government have done their review
Now we have 'the rule of six'
Makes no difference to those selfish pricks
Who do not know or do not care
That others are living in despair
As long as they can go on the piss
Whilst others stare into the abyss
They march in protest, their democratic right
To show their frustration and talk their shite
To spout their blinkered hypocrisy
So 43,000 dead is just a conspiracy?
They strut around they are immune
Anyway, the oldies would have died pretty soon
Let's have normal life quickly restored
With this lockdown thing I'm getting bored
What's a few thousand fatalities
As long as I can resume my activities

26th September 2020

I asked my four-year-old grandson what poems he would like for his bedtime reading. This is the first one, the subject matter was his choice!

Alfie's Adventures - The Gigantic Pump Machine

Our little Alfie is a wonderful lad
Mostly good and rarely bad
If I would have to think of something
It would be his habit of frequently pumping

It must come from his Daddy it would seem
Whose windy problems are more extreme
The worst place in the house I would think
Is in his office, now that does stink

Mummy thought she'd had enough
Of those enormous smelly puffs
Making the air always smell of poo
I must think of something I can do

I think I should buy a massive fan
To blow the smell away if it can
This would clean the air so well
You'd never know there'd been a smell

She put it in Daddy's office upstairs
He wasn't looking so he was unawares
Until he opened the door to a mighty gust
And it blew him over to his disgust

She had to come up with another plan
I need some help if you can
Help me come up with an idea
To get this smell out of here

Alfie said lets have some flowers
It'll make the room smell nice for hours
She placed them there with such pride
But the smell was so bad they soon died

I think I might have a fix
It' a special diet from Joe Wicks
It's stopped the air bubbling in his tum
And those awful smells coming from his bum

So if you detect a little smell
From whom it comes we can tell
It will be from our little lad
And nothing to do with his poor Dad
27th September 2020

Today is my wife Joyce's birthday.

26
Happy Birthday

Another year passes but we remain the stronger
The story of our happiness is getting ever longer
We stride along and fill our lives with joy
Every passing moment we will still enjoy
As another year passes but that is just the way
It's not about how many but how you fill your day

28th September 2020

My sister always writes to me in 'text language' which takes me a little while to translate. I wrote this for her in genuine text language, I consulted a text dictionary, yes there is one, to ensure I got it right.

See if you can understand it?

27
Txt Book Communication

i woz goin 2 rite a letr but i havnt got the time
so i thote i wud txt and acc do it all in rime
its all new to me tbh but i promise ill tc
spose i cud hav done a vm and a msg we cud share
i will blates call u ltr so can u cmb
or maybe fb and i will brb
wotever you choose idc it is nbd
n2m depends how u feel
i havnt mastered txt yet
so WYSIWYG
no diss but maybe its easier 2 m.i.r.l l8r
wen our chance of understanding might be a little
gr8er

28th September 2020

Another 'thought download' about the ageing process,
maybe because it was my wife's birthday yesterday?

28
Tipping Point

It didn't creep up on me, I was watching all along
This was a battle I was determined to prolong
It moved slowly at first but then increased its pace
What started as a stroll now looking more like a race
Dad set the bar pretty low that was my first milestone
His modest achievement now carved on his headstone
Birthdays came and went with cause for celebrations
But not as funny when you did the calculations
A mark of growing up facing the world without fear
Now it's just a reminder that you are indeed still here
The balance shifts all too soon starts to tip the scales
With less in front than behind and all that that entails
There is a certain truth in the saying to I must admit
The toilet roll runs out faster the less there's left on it

28th September 2020

The second in the series of bedtime poems for Alfie

29

Alfie's Adventures – The Birthday Party

It soon will be my birthday
This time I will be four
Mum said I could have my pals round
Maybe six or more

I made my list of friends
Some very special guests
I think it's fair to say
She wasn't that impressed

I invited my friend the lion
But he isn't coming any more
Mum said he's too frightening
With his enormous roar

The snake was next he's okay
But Mum was in a dither
She said he was too slimy
As he would slide and slither

What about a chimp I said
He'd be lots of fun
Mum said we've got a monkey
My sister is the one

Maybe then an elephant
Swinging his huge trunk
But the house is far too small
For such a massive hunk

I'm getting short of ideas
So I suggested a giraffe
Mum said that's too tall
Please don't make me laugh

I've got a plan for Rosie
It might just keep her calmer
I saw it at the zoo
It was called a Llama

The guest list has got shorter
Mum says I'm being silly
The only animal at the party
Is gonna be our Billy

29th September 2020

Another in Alfie's series of bedtime poems.
Alfie loves the planets, so I attempted to write
something that was amusing but mildly educational,
well at least I learnt something in writing it.

30

Alfie's Adventures – Into Space

I would like to see all the planets
When I ask my Mummy smiles
Getting there and back
Would be 6 billion miles

I've already chosen the first one
It's going to be the moon
It really can't be far away
I can see it from my bedroom

Next stop will be Venus
For sure we will not freeze
By the time we get there
It will be at least 800 degrees

Now we have got going
We can venture amongst the stars
We'll set our rocket on course
To land ourselves on Mars

Mercury is a strange one
Where the days they last forever
Though I would like to stay there
I think I might get tired however

Now Jupiter is quite different
Where days pass in a flash
A day only last 10 hours
So I will surely have to dash

Seeing the planet Saturn
Will be one of my favourite things
A planet made just of gas
And those amazing rings

Next stop is Uranus
I'm not sure it will be nice
It's going to be extremely cold
Cause it is made of ice

The furthest plant is Neptune
The last stop for what it's worth
It also is the coldest
And 3 billion miles from Earth

2nd October 2020

The final poem in Alfie's bedtime poem series

31
Bobby Burp

Bobby is a little boy who loves his food and drink
He can eat and drink more than almost anybody I can think
He sits there with his meals and loves to swallow and slurp
Then when his tummy is completely full he lets rip a huge
burp

Now Bobby had a party but he was the only guest
So with an enormous buffet he was truly blessed
Eating all the food for him was obviously a must
And he ate and ate until his belly was very close to bust

But very soon after he did not feel well at all
His tummy was twice the size and very overfull
With the pain first he grimaced then he grinned
It wasn't that he was happy he was just so full of wind

He tried to do some burping but nothing would come out
The pain in his tummy made him scream and shout
If he couldn't shift this wind he would surely bust
Or before much longer he would probably combust

Then he heard it thunder the ground began to shake
Everyone was sure there must be an earthquake
But Bobby felt much better, his tummy now reduced
It wasn't really thunder but the burp he'd just produced

Now Bobby is more careful how much he has to eat
Just enough to make him full, just dinner and a sweet
And he is not so greedy as to get himself all bloated
His terrible wind and sore tummy are now all surely sorted

7th October 2020

My first attempt at writing a limerick.

32
Alfie Meets His Match

There was a little boy called Alfie
Who tried to be a bit bossy
He tried it with sister Rosie
Who said don't be dozy
Nobody messes with me!

7ᵗʰ October 2020

My brother developed early onset
Alzheimer's disease some years ago. I was imagining
what it must feel like as he looks out on his world.

33
Looking Out

If you see me wandering down your street
Just pass on quietly, please don't speak
I am on a journey to who knows where
A voice in my head said I must go there

I talk to those people in my past
Most of whom have long since passed
They are as clear as day I can to see
In my head they're so real to me

I'm on a train to some destination
Can't get off there are no stations
This was not a train I chose to ride
Watching life fly by, on the outside

The paths I take in my mind
Have no real direction I can find
The clarity my thinking needs
Is tangled up in all the weeds

I know I cause so much frustration
But it's dark in here, no illumination
The person you see, you might not recognise
I only wish I could just apologise
And become the person I was before
This terrible thing knocked on our door

7ᵗʰ October 2020

I wrote this after downing my multiple vitamin tablets
one morning.

34
Vitamin Sea

As every year passes I've upped my vitamin doses
Trying to avoid the risk of some terrible diagnoses
It started with just one or two, but it has now grown
I'm now drowning in them, it's becoming overblown

Omega 3 they reckon never disappoints
So now I take triple strength for my aching joints
Glucosamine they recommend for my arthritic knuckles
My wife thinks its all bullshit and it makes her chuckle

That horrible yellow spice will stop me getting sick
So it's two tablets a day full of turmeric
To keep my bones and teeth generally trouble free
It's a small dose every morning of Vitamin D3

To keep my heart ticking and beating right on time
It's a very strange concoction called Q10 Coenzyme
An additional dose of heart health it reckons to supply
An oriental sounding pill with the strange name of Kwai

50 mg Zinc offers so much versatility
Skin, hair and bones and even improved fertility
And finally the last one that costs a pretty penny
I think it's just tomatoes, but they call it Lycopene

There was a time I recall when I was such a fine specimen
I never even thought I needed any kind of vitamin
Surely my morning dosage will be my salvation
But I get up so early I'm suffering sleep deprivation

11th October 2020

A comment on how we should try and keep an
enquiring mind as we get older.

35
Human Racing

Reaching the final laps of the human race
How much should we drop the pace
Surely we should prize the fun and laughter
There ain't much of that in the hereafter
Don't let perceived injustice burn and smoulder
Increasing the weight of that chip on your shoulder
New experiences we can still create
Not allowing our mind to insulate
Us from the pleasures and joy of today
Or a high price we will surely pay
Letting our Autumn days just drift by
With a long face and a weary sigh
With a heavy heart, the spark extinguished
Dropping out early the race unfinished

11th October 2020

A poem I wrote as an introduction to one of the
chapters in my autobiography describing our move to
our current home in Clophill.

36
Our Country House

Many streets we had to roam
To find a place we could call home
It lacked finesse with not much style
But this was our very own country pile
Many hours of toil and sweat
Until expectations were really met
A new side of us this did invoke
As we became proper village folk

11th October 2020

A reaction to the news that Donald Trump (allegedly)
had Covid-19

37
Trumped Up

I'm surprised it took so long you might ask
As the cocky buffoon wouldn't wear a mask
Thank God the virus hasn't caught us
But it predictably tracked down the esteemed POTUS

If you disagree you're a scaremonger
The Donald said he felt 20 years younger
So if you're getting a bit long in the tooth
Covid is now the elixir of youth

Scores of doctors came to his aid
To make sure he made it to his motorcade
To wave his hand and hear them cheer
His bodyguards huddled far too near

I beat the virus he now gloats
Just get out there and cast your votes
All doom-laden claims must be rejected
As long as this lunatic gets re-elected

11th October 2020

No one on the BBC can wind me up quite as much as the inherently biased and negative Laura Kuenssburg.

38
Oh Laura

Tune in tonight for the BBC news
For a generous serving of left wing views
The aggressive stance of Ms Kuenssburg
About as much appeal as a warm Carlsberg

That whining voice and wiry smile
Enough to make you run a mile
Self-important cocky aura
That's what you get with our Laura

Yes she has another question
Full of all her negative suggestion
Cold as the proverbial iceberg
A humourless soul Laura Kuenssburg

Working hard to catch them out
With all her journalistic clout
One dimensional and bound to bore ya
Please give us a break for God's sake Laura

13th October 2020

Just a bit of light relief.

39
Never A Cross Word –
Just Guess The 10 Groups

Are these guys from the Fylde Coast
As keeping off the rain seems to matter the most

Coming from the desert their name depicts
But I rather think it is up the M6

Their great rivals struggled to see
How they might end up living in the country

These songs you're feelings they can skew
These boys can easily make you blue

This heavy mob caused more than a blip
As they launched their musical airship

They could have come from a religious place
But more likely Jordyland is the case

A mega group that spawned an era
Bad spellers that derive from the Coleoptera

A physcodelic foursome out in space
Singing about the black part of this place

Don't leave me now in Illinois
The life by a great lake that we enjoy

My sibling he is not at all overweight
And us lads from Manchester will not berate

Answers Overleaf

Answers

Fleetwood Mac, Oasis, Blur, Moody Blues,
Lindisfarne, Led Zeppelin, The Beatles, Pink
Floyd, Chicago, The Hollies

13th October 2020

I was thinking of all the cars I had owned in my life,
most of the good ones being company cars. I think this
is a complete list give or take.

40
Who's Gonna Drive You Home Tonight?

My first car, a Viva so sleek and white
Shame the chassis was rusted like shite
Another Viva in bottle green
Dad sprayed it up and made it gleam
Australia brought a Rootes Estate
Blew the engine driving interstate
Tony sold me a Viva in striking gold
Looked like new, a joy to behold
A Morris Marina another family bequest
But British Leyland at it's best
A company car a gift as if from Santa
A sexy beast the Opel Manta
A shitty bucket that tiny Colt
United Co-op gave my ego a jolt
My first new car, a red Cavalier
Marked an upturn in my career
A green Cavalier next in line
This style of car suited us fine
A bronze metallic Renault Estate
New family status did dictate
Promotion brought the Renault Monaco
Fancy car to go with the dough
Next came some class I have to say
A BMW 5 with which to play
The A5 coupe was very sporty
Looking cool was my forte
Mercedes C top of the range
Different car just for a change
BMW 5 a grey estate
More suited my family state
Another Merc in sexy turquoise
Very smart with sporty alloys
E Class Mercs were now for me
I stuck with them and then had three
The Beamers came back very soon
Blinding white and then maroon
The sleek Calibra went too far
Couldn't get the kids in the car
A couple of more Beamers at my new work
With a Merc thrown in as a perk
Now we drive the BM classic
No more free cars, that ain't fantastic

14th October 2020

Something of an ode to being brought up in a the North
of England in a very working class family

41
Job for Life

Northern grit running through the veins
Of working folk with labour pains
A job for life is what we need
With all these hungry mouths to feed

Don't try and get above your station
As aspiration drowns in perspiration
Working class morals must prevail
As watching eyes wait for you to fail

People like us don't crave success
We have no real desire to progress
Thoughts of change that could come to pass
We're Northern folk and working class

15th October 2020

A short poem remembering our wedding day.

42
Getting Hitched

Gathered together family and friends
Those dodgy flares, those eighties trends
Lovely gifts and wedding flowers
Photos snapped whilst dodging showers

Seven years on and now we're hitched
Sharing our vows our lives enriched
We took the walk up yonder aisle
A reason for us all to smile

Raise your glasses and make a toast
Husband and wife, we can boast
And make our plans for coming years
But just for now let's share a few beers

15th October 2020

I wrote this as a little educational poem for grandson
Alfie

43
Alpabetti Spaghetti

A is for Alfie, a grand little lad
B is for Billy who can bark like mad
C is for Crazy, that's what Billy can be
D is for Daddy who looks after me
E is for Elsie now five years old
F is for Faye a princess I'm told
G is for Grandad a really funny one
H is for Hair of which he has none
I is for Issy who is always glad
J is for Jokes my Grandads are bad
K is for Koala an animal of Australian fame
L is for Langhorn because that is my name
M is for Mummy who looks after me
N is for Nanna who is kind as can be
O is for Ollie my cousin down under
P is for Penny a lady of wonder
Q is for Quick as my sister thinks
R is for Rosie the little lovely minx
S is for School where I work and play
T is for Teacher who helps each day
U is for Uncle Rob the man with a van
V is another Van that's the Amazon man
W is for Work my Daddy does upstairs
X is for X-Rays Mummy does at hers
Y is for Yoghurt for after my tea
Z is for Zoo a great day out for me

19ᵗʰ October 2020

I am not a fan of the banal rubbish that often appears
on Facebook,

44
Facebook Warrior

From behind my screen at a stroke
So much controversy I try to stoke
Highlight injustice wherever it might hide
Without having to get off my backside

Just a like or a crafty share
This Facebook Warrior can be there
No actual effort do I engage
As my conscience I can assuage

My comments I know no one can trace
As they end all end up in cyberspace
Why do I engage in this pantomime
Surely it's just a complete waste of time

Any change is surely an illusion
Does any of this bring different conclusion
The impact I make is surely a myth
I'm just feeding another corporate monolith

A different outcome might come to pass
If you actually got up off your ass
Abandon those pathetic internet factions
And back your concerns with some concrete actions

20th October 2020

One of those rather depressing age-related poems

45

Days of Future Passed

Making plans for what lies ahead
Will it be joy or will it be dread
Guaranteeing I see my plans play out
Always contains a scintilla of doubt

An oft made quip from us older folk
A real anxiety wrapped in a joke
Said with almost comedic fear
"That would be nice if I'm still here"

It's very plain for all to see
My future is surely now behind me
No summer sun or gentle breeze
Can ever blow away this unease

The reality might be unpalatable
That the future path is inevitable
So enjoy the moment fill your day
Don't let precious time just fade away

22nd October 2020

We had just come off the phone to our friends in France and I wrote this for them. The place they are staying is called Tourne Sol which is French for sunflower.

46
Tourne Sol

Our own little haven across the pond
Of which we have quickly grown so fond
It's tranquil setting such healing power
Our precious yellow French sunflower

A peaceful wander on a canal side walk
Friendly chitchat and amusing small talk
Days out driving classic cars
Coffee and cake in Gallic bars

Morning walks seventeen thousand steps
Weary legs and tired triceps
The boulangère keeps us well fed
With a daily ration of luscious French bread

Newfound friends as well as neighbours
Certainly beats the management labours
Of the daily demands of a stroppy boss
And a moaning workforce who don't give a toss

A peaceful life devoid of stress
Seems immune from a world in such a mess
Such time together we're never bored
We are simply finding our lost chord

23rd October 2020

I had an appointment in Bedford town centre, I was
shocked at how the town had declined with the closure
of so many shops.

47
Ghost Town

Whitewashed windows no display
Nothing to buy so nothing to pay
Cheap discount shops are all that remain
Going out shopping will never be the same
Just a few drunks sat on a bench
Smoke in the air and a boozy stench
Finding somewhere open is such task
And even then you will need your mask
Save the work and save some time
Everything's available on Amazon Prime
The Specials lyrics had it nailed down
This town is coming like a ghost town

25th October 2020

I hate the winter darkness and I wrote this the day the clocks went back.

48
SAD Day

The darkness came fast, almost overnight
The end of summer like switching a light
No more sitting in the evening sun
Those balmy days are all but done

Every day it creeps up faster
The weather's grim says the weather forecaster
You better move quickly or you will see
It could be pitch black by half past three

As if you aren't already veering off track
It's October and the clocks go back
Close the blinds and have you tea
Now all there you've got is crap TV

Nothing's changed but I must combat
The feeling that my battery's flat
I need some warmth a little sun
Wishing time away till winters done

25th October 2020

I wrote this thinking about how people often just let their days drift by without the motivation to actually get up and do something positive with their time.

49
Nothing to do but Today

Woke up this morning there was no alarm
I'll stay here a while it will do no harm
There's no panic, I think I'll just lay
With nothing to do, but today

No real pressure no schedule to meet
Just chill out and put up my feet
I'm not that busy it's just my way
Really nothing to do, but today

Talk to my friends let's take a look
I know where they are they're all on Facebook
Their conversation won't lead me astray
I have nothing to do, but today

Turn on the TV make a selection
Anything will do I have no direction
Their grim messages they will certainly convey
They have nothing to do, but today

So much I could do but let's just get real
Sitting here drifting is just how I feel
So little to do and even less to say
There's nothing to do, but today

So many opportunities but I lack motivation
I won a medal for procrastination
Any new plans I will have to delay
As I have nothing to do, but today

26th October 2020

A short limerick dedicated to our neighbour at Blakeney

50
A Clean Sweep

A caravaner who sold cars for Honda
Of his wife he couldn't be fonder
Whilst he was sweeping his decking
She would always be checking
To the next job his mind didn't wander

27th October 2020

I was talking to somebody about moving roles at work
and it made me think about what we often called
friendships at work but in reality do not endure after
the work relationship is gone.

51
Did We Pass Somewhere?

Long days and hours of relentless work
From the challenge we never did shirk
But we were such a great team
Above all others we reigned supreme

All for one and one for all
In the business we stood so tall
Such friendships that could not be broken
Our commitment to each other simply unspoken

Things may not be like they appear
Those friends we made in our long career
Now they are just not the same
Not sure they even remember my name

Some recognition you might think was owed
But those close bonds so quickly erode
And the reality is laid completely bare
"Do I remember you, did we pass somewhere?"

3rd November 2020

As we enter another lockdown I penned this little rhyme

52
Homeward Bound

Boris is at it again
Your gonna be locked in your pen
Not everyone agrees
We should fight this disease
Especially rich businessmen

My friend thinks it's all a hoax
And the government is conning us folks
But there is a warning
From the thousands in mourning
It's a hell of a risk and no joke

We cannot shop for a while
So everybody's gonna stockpile
I blow a fuse
When I see all the queues
That clog up every shopping aisle

Now here is the real rub
Nobody can go to the pub
For the resourceful few
It's a drop of home brew
Drinking while in the bath tub

Is that a knock on the door I hear
Can't be anybody that I hold dear
I know I'm a worrier
But it's only a courier
Bringing me more of my Amazon gear

We are all counting the days
When we can back to normal ways
Let the winter intervene
Till we get a vaccine
And forget this horrible phase

3rd November 2020

We were just talking to our friend in France who has
escaped the UK lockdown to enjoy a rather well-earned
but rather eccentric long holiday.

53
Lost in France

Whilst I'm loving my time here in France
This language is leading me a merry dance
Some of these words are so obscure
The only French word I know is bonjour

I always greet the locals with a smile
But they just seem to stare at me awhile
My vocabulary limited that's for sure
But I always respond politely with a bonjour

With French fashion I'm trying to flirt
I've even cut the sleeves off my shirt
I'm trying to be all haute couture
To expand my repertoire from just bonjour

Even Amber seems to have been stricken
She's walking round with a toy dead chicken
She's normally relaxed and quite demur
Now her bark even sounds like bonjour

She's not alone I must concede
The other dog has been christened Weed
The Gendarmerie might be interested I am sure
We might soon be hearing bonjour bonjour bonjour

5th November 2020

My brother who is currently unwell had a setback last night, this was my reflection this morning.

54
The Stranger

A crazy man is in our street
Long hair and a wild beard
Not the kind you like to meet
He's clearly slightly weird

A distant look in empty eyes
No sign of recognition
Keep your distance I'd advise
He's clearly on a mission

Some people gather to assist
And help this man calm down
But all their efforts he resists
As he marches up and down

I think I know who he might be
We were close to one another
Beneath the madness I now see
He used to be my brother

That bond I know I can't revive
His normal life in mortal danger
The person I knew is no longer alive
This man is now a stranger

5th November 2020

The news is pretty grim at the moment so I was looking for inspiration to look at the brighter side of life

55
An Ode to Ian Dury
– Reasons To Be Cheerful?

America divided, no result can be decided
The electorate misguided, streets will be ablaze
Lockdown last forever, all of our endeavour
No freedom whatsoever, just more delays

Long queues they are a forming, no one is conforming
TV misinforming, the truth they betray
Half the country's on furlough, bit hard to swallow
Economy being hollowed, who will pay
No pub drinking, what must they be thinking
Stomachs will be shrinking, change our ways
I'm not going to worry, no need to scurry
We're not in a hurry, it's just a phase

Reasons to be cheerful 123

Captain Tom a hero, walks again with gusto
Old man's got his mojo, whilst we're in a daze
NHS workers, none of them are shirkers
Such caretakers, so full of praise
Go for a walk, hear the birds squawk
Chat and talk, on Autumn days
Late morning waking, more news is breaking
Cakes you are baking, beautiful buffets
Hours spent on Facetime, make up a new rhyme
Glass of red wine, a cabernet
Jo Wicks exercising, stop us oversizing
The pain is agonising, it's just a craze

Reasons to be cheerful 123

5th November 2020

I wrote this to celebrate the birth of my nephew's new baby son, Charlie.

56
Boys Zone

A bundle of joy our precious new-born
A beautiful addition to family Langhorn
Little Charlie such a grand little lad
Just as handsome as his old Dad
A complete family for Hayley and Matt
To make their perfect habitat
Their dear Mother now clearly outnumbered
As the boys club grows unencumbered
The lady of the house all alone
In what is Australia's own Boy Zone

6th November 2020

Watching the debacle that is the US election, I had to put
pen to paper.

57
Having a 'Tantrump'

Its just not fair I let them vote
To keep my burgeoning ego afloat
This is really too hard to take
There must be a big mistake

I'll kick and scream whatever they say
Until I eventually get my own way
I refuse to let them dismiss
The world's biggest narcissist

Putting all logic aside
I expected it to be a landslide
With the vote they've dabbled
To get rid of the great Donald

They may think they've won by a few
But I am definitely going to sue
I don't care if I'm not acting adult
I will never accept this result

In the world's biggest democracy
I know this looks like lunacy
But I am just too great
Not to be the head of this state

I will pursue my own agenda
Despite embarrassing America
As long as this abates
This is anything but the 'United' States

7th November 2020

I was reflecting on how Jeff Bezos had become the new
Father Christmas.

58
A New Santa

Long gone the days of Santa's Sleigh
In 2020 we have a new way
To save the reindeer being on cue
Or Santa getting stuck in the flue
No mince pies on the windowsill
No Christmas stockings he needs to fill
Christmas shopping a thing of the past
New Santa's job a sharp contrast
As restriction have been imposed
All the shops are now closed
Just a phone and the easy App
Write to Santa at a tap
Everything delivered just on time
Not from Lapland but Amazon Prime

7th November 2020

It's a beautiful Autumn morning as I look out of my window.

59
Autumn Days

Summer days have slipped away
Clocks jumped forward a shorter day
A gentle frost in the morning
Of colder days a subtle warning
Golden backdrop of Autumn leaves
A stunning vista it effortlessly weaves
Country walks all wrapped up warm
The bracing air will do no harm
Darker evenings spent around the fire
An extra layer you might require
Beneath the covers snuggled up in bed
Keeping warm a good book read
Winter beckons Christmas cheer
Before you know it Spring is here

8th November 2020

Today is Remembrance Sunday, conducted whilst we are
all under a second national lockdown.

60
Lest We Forget

So many people rue their plight
Their favourite pub closed every night
These rules they say are too much to bear
Constraining their freedom is just not fair

Their protests rather quickly fade
Compared to those whose lives were laid
Down for all our freedom today
A sacrifice we should never betray

On this another Remembrance Day
We carry a debt we can't repay
Let's think of those who now have no voice
So we could have so much choice

8th November 2020

We continue to witness the bizarre behaviour of the outgoing President of the United States. I thought I would have a go at his beloved tweeting

61
Tweet Tweet

President Trump, came down with a bump

Joe Biden, gave him a bit of a hiding

In every tweet, he denies defeat

A challenge he's mounting, citing serious miscounting

He continues to moan, from his White House home

Trump's bitter indeed, no intention to concede

Rather than endorse, spends his time on his golf course

He'll use legal means, to fight on it seems

I'VE BEEN CHEATED, the President Tweeted

9th November 2020

The announcement came out this evening about a
potential new Covid vaccine, good news at last.

62
Have I Got News for You?

Is this the day we were waiting for
To kick this damn virus out the door
So we can recover ordinary life at last
That we so took for granted in the past

Put an end to this ruinous lockdown
Get back to work open up my town
Give us a shot at normal life
And end the conflict and the strife

At first it might only be the few
But we patiently in the queue
Till the obvious benefits can be seen
Of this new hopeful new Covid vaccine

Maybe we can dump the mask and visor
Thanks to the work of a group called Pfizer
So let's get out of the starting blocks
And put this disease back in its box

14ᵗʰ November 2020

There is a sense we might just be turning a corner in our
fight against the pandemic.

63
All Things Must Pass

This journey it seems to never end
More danger lurking around the bend
Just when a light begins to glimmer
Another statistic makes things go dimmer

Don't lose hope because alas
You must believe, all things must pass

Surely all this effort will pay back
And repel the enemy's relentless attack
So many good people taking care
Hoping for normality if we dare

Our best efforts we can surpass
In the knowledge, all things must pass

The magic bullet should soon be here
Extinguishing this overwhelming fear
Greater enemies we have overcome
Finding courage we will not succumb

Our collective effort we must amass
To ensure, all things must pass

Our children will look back in awe
At the stress and suffering that they saw
When the world came under attack
But humanity found its way back

Kick out this visitor that did trespass
See it off, all things must pass

Auld Lang Syne sings his tune
This terrible year can't end too soon
Roll on into twenty- twenty one
And hope and pray it's a better one

We will break this deadly impasse
And look forward again, all things must pass

14th November 2020

And finally............

64
A Dusty Old Book

One day while rummaging in the attic
Just passing time nothing dramatic
I came upon some paraphernalia
An old stamp album, an encyclopaedia
I dug down to take a closer look
And found a rather old dusty book
It told of family and good times
In serious poetry and amusing rhymes
Of a terrible disease that stopped the world
As its terrible impact ruthlessly unfurled
Of political argument on either side
Whilst tens of thousands sadly died
Wearing masks and standing clear
Of anyone who dare stand too near
At times it must have been really sad
In those old days of my Grandad

15th November 2020

Postscript

65
That's It For Now

That dear embattled wife of mine
Was fed up of me talking in rhyme
I was so metronomic
She so needed a tonic
She stuck my poetry book where the sun don't shine

Printed in Great Britain
by Amazon

54484252R00079